NEO-CLASSICAL DESIGN
CD-ROM AND BOOK

Charles Normand

DOVER PUBLICATIONS, INC.
Mineola, New York

The CD-ROM on the inside back cover contains all of the images shown in the book. There is no installation necessary. Just insert the CD into your computer and call the images into your favorite software (refer to the documentation with your software for further instructions). Each image has been scanned at 600 dpi and saved in six different formats—BMP, EPS, GIF, JPEG, PICT, and TIFF. The JPEG and GIF files—the most popular graphics file types used on the Web—are Internet-ready.

The "Images" folder on the CD contains a number of different folders. All of the TIFF images have been placed in one folder, as have all of the PICT, all of the EPS, etc. The images in each of these folders are identical except for file format. Every image has a unique file name in the following format: xxx.xxx. The first 3 or 4 characters of the file name, before the period, correspond to the number printed with the image in the book. The last 3 characters of the file name, after the period, refer to the file format. So, 001.TIF would be the first file in the TIFF folder.

Also included on the CD-ROM is Dover Design Manager, a simple graphics editing program for Windows that will allow you to view, print, crop, and rotate the images.

For technical support, contact:
Telephone: 1 (617) 249-0245
Fax: 1 (617) 249-0245
Email: dover@artimaging.com
Internet: **http://www.dovertechsupport.com**
The fastest way to receive technical support is via email or the Internet.

Bibliographical Note

Neo-Classical Design CD-ROM and Book, first published in 2005, contains all of the plates from *Le Guide de L'Ornemaniste ou de L'Ornement,* by Charles Normand, published in Paris in 1826.

Dover Electronic Clip Art ®

International Standard Book Number: 0-486-99696-4

Manufactured in the United States of America
Dover Publications, Inc., 31 East 2nd Street, Mineola, N.Y. 11501

002

003

004

2

005

006

007

3

009

010

011

6

013

014

015

016

017

018

019

020

021

022

023

024

025

026

027

028

029

030

031

032

033

034

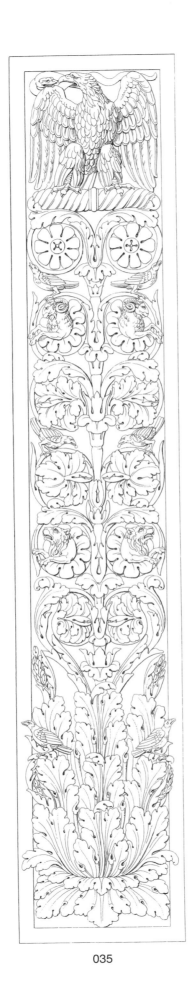

035

036

039

040

041

042

044

043

045

046

047

048

049

051

052

053

22

054

055

056

057

23

058

059

060

061

062

24

065

066

067

068

069

070

072

073

074

075

076

077

079

080

081

082

083

084

085

086

087

088

089

090

091

092

093

095

096

097

098

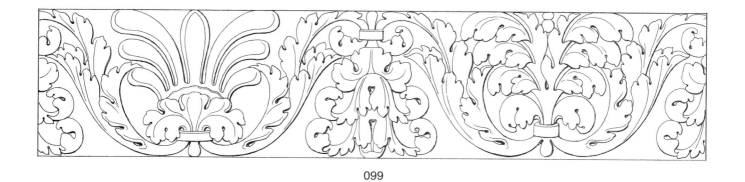

099

100

35

101

102

103

104

105

106

107

108

109

110

111

112

113

114

115

116

117

118

119

120

121

122

123

124

125

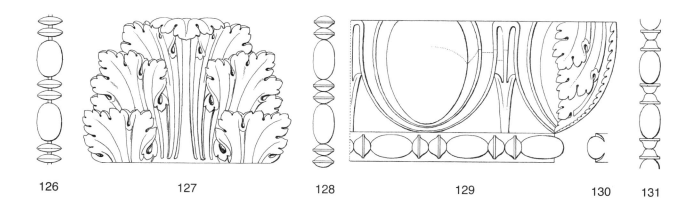

126   127   128   129   130   131

132

133

134

135

136

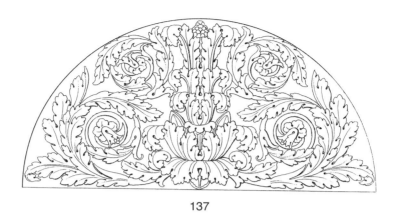

137

138

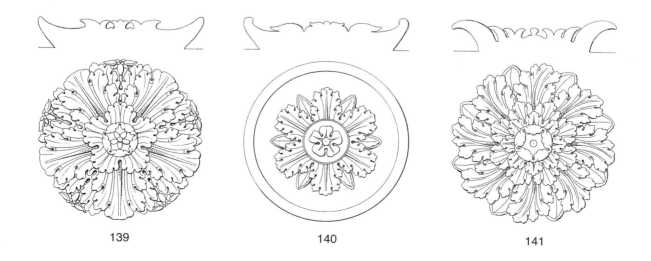

139

140

141

142

143

144

145

146

147

148

43

149

150

151

152

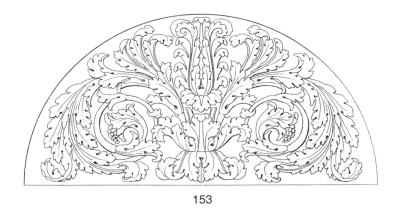

153

154

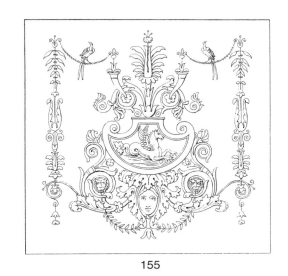

155

156